Home Pasta Top Tips

Smith Family Retail

1st Edition February 2014

Smith Family Retail

Copyright © 2014 Andrew Smith (Smith Family Retail)
contact@smithfamilyretail.com

All rights reserved.

ISBN: 1496007336
ISBN-13: 978-1496007339

Contents

How this book works — 1

Flour — 2

Dough Recipes — 4

Noodle Dough Recipes — 10

Kneading Technique — 12

Cutting — 15

Drying — 17

Storing — 20

Cooking — 22

Recipes — 24

How this book works

If you want top tips fast, this book can be read in minutes!

Simply read the first paragraph of each section. Top tips in seconds. You can't miss these paragraphs, they are bold and large font.

If you want a more detailed explanation of the section, then keep reading.

For those of you who are already home experts, much of this will be a refresher with hopefully a few gems thrown in. We hope you find this little book a big help.

Most importantly - have fun creating your own secret family recipe!

Flour

The protein in flour is called gluten. The 'harder' the flour, the more gluten, the better it holds together and fewer eggs are needed.

00 is fine soft flour and requires eggs in the recipe.

Bread flour is a strong flour and is often used for pasta dough even without eggs.

Before we start, here is a word on flour. It may all look the same, but it's not! The way flour behaves depends largely on the protein % and which parts of the grain are in it. As you read below just know gluten is the protein in flour. Here is a summary of some of the flours you might use for pasta.

All-Purpose Flour - has a moderate amount of gluten, and therefore produces tougher dough. As refined flour it has no bran or wheat germ to affect its softness.

Strong Flour - a good strong bread flour is commonly used for pasta making. There is enough strength in the gluten meaning the pasta can be made even without eggs. The eggs however will make a richer pasta.

OO Flour - is the flour purists use. It is a very fine soft flour. It is low in gluten and because of this the pasta needs something to hold it together. Recipes with OO Flour need the eggs to perform this task.

O Flour - is halfway between a strong flour and the OO. It has more gluten and requires fewer eggs than the OO Flour. Sometimes it is used as a blend with stronger flour such as Durum. Basically, the stronger the flour the fewer eggs required.

Durum Flour - is a very hard high gluten flour. Typically not used on its own in home baking, it is more commonly used commercially to blend with softer flours.

Semolina - is very high in gluten. Durum Wheat Semolina is used commercially for making dried pasta as no egg is required. This makes the manufacturing handling process simpler. At home it isn't generally used on its own as it can be difficult to handle. It can be mixed with other softer flour.

Dough Recipes

If you just want to get started, the simplest recipe is approximately 1 egg for every ½ cup (100g/3.5oz) flour.

Basic

[approximately 1 egg to ½ cup (100g/3.5oz) flour]

4 eggs

1 ⅔ (400g/14oz) flour

Standard

[approximately 1 egg to ½ cup (100g/3.5oz) flour]

4 eggs

1 ⅔ (400g/14oz) flour

pinch of salt

1 tsp extra virgin olive oil

Traditional

1 ⅔ cups (400g/14oz) flour

or half flour and half semolina flour (called farina di semola or Italian durum wheat flour)

2 eggs

1 tablespoon olive oil

pinch of sea salt

Gluten Free Flour

1 cup (240g/8.5oz) gluten-free flour (already has xantham gum & behaves like regular flour)

1 egg

2 tbsp milk

½ tsp baking powder

½ tsp salt

Simple Gluten Free

1 cup (100g/3.5oz) chickpea flour

1 egg

you **must** add salt to the water when cooking this pasta

Gluten Free

1 cup (125g/4.4oz) tapioca flour

1 cup (125g/4.4oz) corn starch

⅓ cup (60g/2oz) potato starch

1 ½ tsp salt

1 tbsp guar gum or xanthan gum

Complex Gluten Free

⅔ cup (70g/2.5oz) corn flour

½ cup (70g/2.5oz) quinoa flour

½ cup (60g/2.1oz) potato starch

2 tsp xanthan gum

1 tsp guar gum

1 tsp fine sea salt

2 large eggs

4 egg yolks from large eggs

Herb Dough

Simply wash and dry some Italian Parsley, Dill, Tarragon or Cilantro. Chop finely and add sparingly to the dough when mixing.

Yellow Dough

Depending on the size and consistency of your mix, simply add an egg yolk. Alternatively replace some of the eggs with egg yolks. You may need to add a little water or olive oil to replace the moisture content in the dough.

Green Dough

Wash some spinach, shred and while just wet pop it into a pot to heat and wilt. Add a pinch of salt. It should take about 5 minutes.

Once it is cooled, squeeze as much water out as you can. Blend it up and use it with the other ingredients when you mix your dough. Simple!

Red Dough

Dice and slowly cook carrots in salted water. Drain the water from the pot and add tomato paste. You just heat this, stirring constantly to remove the moisture content.

When it is quite firm, simply cool and add to the other ingredients when you mix your dough. Simple!

Noodle Dough Recipes

Trying to replicate authentic Asian noodles outside of Asia is a tough ask. However there are some obvious substitutions.

Italian Pastas make good stand-ins for egg and wheat flour noodles. Which one you choose depends on the shape of the noodle you are replacing. Thin angel hair pasta can be used for cellophane noodles, and fettuccine as a replacement for wheat flour noodles.

Egg Noodles

Any of the standard pasta recipes with high egg content are effectively an egg noodle. You can make and use in Asian dishes at home.

Rice Noodles

3 ¼ cups (400g/14oz) tapioca flour

3 ½ cups (460g/16oz) white rice flour (not glutinous rice flour)

4 or 5 cups boiling water (it must be boiling!)

extra tapioca flour for rolling out

extra water to add when nearly mixed

Kneading Technique

Use a food processor with the cutting blade. Mix ingredients until they resemble bread crumbs.

Knead by pushing down and away with your palm, fold and turn 90 degrees and repeat until you have a smooth silky texture.

Break into balls, wrap in plastic wrap and leave to rest for at least 30 minutes.

Kneading pasta and noodle dough is a skill anyone can master. It's not difficult but it is hard work!

First tip here is start with a food processor. Purists may be screaming at this point. Let them scream. It is far easier in the early stages of mixing the dough to throw the eggs and flour into the processor. Just with the normal cutting blade. Let it do the work until the contents look like breadcrumbs.

Tip the dough crumbs onto a bench, previously wiped with flour so they don't stick. Then use your hands to bring them together. Start off by just squishing them into a ball. Don't worry you haven't missed out on all of the hard work.

Now the real part starts. Push down and away on the ball of dough with the fleshy part of your palms. Imagine you are trying to smear the dough across the bench.

Fold the flattened dough and scrunch it to a bit of a ball again.

Turn 90 degrees and repeat the push down and away...repeat!

The idea is to beat the dough up, stretch it, and generally treat it badly. This actually changes the makeup of the mix to develop the gluten in the pasta, which affects how it cooks and feels as a finished product.

It is hard work and you need to keep at it until the feel of the dough changes. You will know when this happens. Instead of pushing around a sandy or gritty ball, suddenly you are smearing a silky smooth substance across the bench.

It feels right, it feels smooth, you will know!

Immediately break into four even balls and wrap with

plastic wrap / Saran wrap. Make sure there are no air bubbles. You don't want dry bits of dough ending up in your beautiful noodles or pasta.

Rest the wrapped up dough for at least 30 minutes. This will make it more elastic.

Cutting

To cut by hand, first roll dough until about 1/16 inch thick. Fold and cut. Untangle noodles and hang on a Home Kitchen Queen pasta drying rack.

To cut by machine, flatten a ball to the size of your hand and feed through the machine changing the setting by one or two each time. Feed through the cutting setting. Hang on a Home Kitchen Queen pasta drying rack.

Fresh pasta can hang for 15-30 minutes before cooking.

Pasta can be cut by hand or by machine. Which process and the desired result is entirely a personal choice.

To cut by hand first you need to roll the pasta out. Taking one of your covered balls of pasta, unwrap and roll out evenly onto a flat surface dusted with flour. You want a nice even thickness of about 1/16 inch (1.6mm).

Then fold like a big flat tube. Cut to the desired width and shake the noodles out to their full length after cutting. The most effective thing to do with your freshly cut pasta is to hang it directly on a Home Kitchen Queen pasta drying rack. Fresh pasta can hang for 15-30 minutes before cooking.

A home pasta cutting machine can really help the process. Take one of your balls and divide if necessary. Flatten a little until you have an oval shape about the size of your hand. You don't want the oval to be too wide to fit through the machine.

Then it is just a case of winding it through the machine, changing the setting by one or two each time making the pasta thinner on each pass.

Change the top component and wind through one last time to cut your pasta or noodles. It is much easier to operate the machine with more than one person. Take the nice long noodles and hang immediately on a Home Kitchen Queen pasta drying rack.

Drying

Hang fresh pasta on a Home Kitchen Queen pasta drying rack for up to 15 to 30 minutes before cooking.

Hang pasta on a Home Kitchen Queen pasta drying rack for 3 to 4 hours or until completely dry ready for storing in air-tight containers.

There are two reasons you may be drying pasta. The first is to dry freshly made pasta enough so it doesn't stick together as a big mess when you cook it.

The second reason is to completely dry pasta to store for long periods of time.

Drying for Cooking Fresh Same Day

If you are cooking pasta the same day, you don't need to dry it out completely. You do however need to stop it sticking together. Spread the pasta evenly along the arms of your Home Kitchen Queen pasta drying rack. Make sure the strands aren't touching. It may take just 5 to 10 minutes depending on the humidity of your region or the weather on the day.

Fresh pasta noodles can be left for up to 15 to 30 minutes before cooking. Now you are ready to cook. *Remember fresh pasta cooks very quickly.*

Drying For Storing

Drying pasta for storing can take just 3 to 4 hours or even up to a day. To store pasta you want it very dry. If there is any moisture left in the pasta and you don't store it in the refrigerator, mold will grow.

The humidity in your region, weather, and thickness of your pasta are all factors for how long it will take to dry. It can be helpful to turn the pasta to dry evenly from both sides.

Also pasta can be dried in direct sunlight. Store the dried pasta in air-tight containers.

There are plenty of things you can try to hang your fresh pasta on. None are more effective than a purpose built Home Kitchen Queen pasta drying rack. Don't make the mistake of going to all the effort of mixing, kneading and cutting your home-made pasta, only to ruin it by hanging it on something that is going to get it dirty or break it.

If you are making and drying pasta often, a purpose built Home Kitchen Queen pasta drying rack is going to save you a lot of grief in the long run. Traditionally families in Italy make and dry large batches of pasta on racks as part of the daily rhythm of life.

Storing

Freeze fresh pasta for keeping for several months. Store in airtight containers with as little air space as possible. This prevents ice crystals forming.

Dry pasta completely to store for 2 to 3 years in air-tight containers. *Remember dried pasta takes longer to cook than fresh or fresh-frozen pasta.*

Pasta or noodles can be stored in two ways.

They can be stored frozen. This is taking fresh pasta or noodles and freezing them. Frozen pasta and noodles maintain their shape and keep their flavor better than dried. Freezing extends life by several months, but eventually you will get freezer burn.

You still need to hang them on a purpose built Home Kitchen Queen pasta drying rack so they don't stick together. Hang for 5-10 minutes in the same way as when you cook them fresh. Store in airtight containers with as little air room as possible. This prevents ice crystals forming on the pasta. Resealable plastic bags are ideal as they can be filled nice and flat, and stacked in the freezer.

Remember fresh pasta and noodles cook faster than dried.

You don't need to thaw your frozen pasta before cooking, and it will hardly affect cooking time.

The alternative is to dry your pasta or noodles completely. This takes 3-4 hours or even up to a day. Removing the moisture content completely means they can be stored for long periods of time without refrigeration. In fact up to 2-3 years. If there is any moisture left in the pasta and you don't store it in the refrigerator, mold will grow.

Pasta and noodles can be dried in direct sunlight. This is intended as a method of preservation first done in the middle east, and is still a method used in factory production of noodles in mainland China. It is advisable to put your Home Kitchen Queen pasta drying rack near a sunny window inside.

Literally putting them outside is going to depend on where you live. You don't want car fumes or dust on your pasta or noodles! Once completely dry, put your pasta or noodles in an airtight container.

Remember dried pasta and noodles take longer to cook, as they need time to absorb water and rehydrate before starting the cooking process.

Cooking

Use a large pot and a lot of water. Add salt until salty as sea-water. Keep the water boiling, add pasta and stir for a minute.

Taste, taste, taste. Keep some of the water for thickening the sauce.

There aren't too many steps in cooking pasta. None of the measurements or times are exact. But there are some definite techniques that will help.

Use an oversize pot to cook pasta. The more water the better. A rough guide is to put 1 gallon of water for every pound of pasta.

Bring the water to the boil then season it. 2-4 tbsp of salt. Pasta water should be salty like the sea.

Keep the water boiling and add the pasta. Gently stir for a minute or so to prevent the pasta sticking together while the gluten forms.

Taste. The only way to tell if your pasta is ready is to taste it. It should be a little firm to the bite. Exactly how firm is going to depend on how you are going to use it.

Drain in a colander but still wet and add to pasta

sauce in a pan to mix. You want this pasta reasonably firm as it is going to continue to cook with the sauce.

Drain well in a colander and return to the empty pot. Add a little olive oil, ready to serve and add sauce on top. This pasta should be a little firm still as it will continue to cook from the heat.

Drain and run cold water over the pasta in the colander. The idea is to stop the cooking process by removing the heat. This is for pasta you are going to use in a pasta salad. This pasta needs to be cooked enough to eat as is.

The best judge of whether your pasta is correctly cooked is you. *Remember dried pasta will take longer to cook* as it needs to rehydrate before the cooking process starts. Don't get caught out, *fresh pasta can cook very quickly, and may only take several minutes in boiling water to be ready.*

Keep some of the pasta water aside. Because this water contains starch from the pasta it can help with the thickening of sauces.

Recipes

We aren't going to attempt to list pasta sauce recipes here. They are as varied as each region and each individual family. There is an endless supply of recipes accessible online for inspiration.

All we will say is that traditional authentic Italian pasta sauces are likely to include a mix of tomatoes, olive oil, basil, garlic, and pepper. Some people may even say that is too many ingredients.

When we start talking about noodles it is just as complex and varied. Different cultures and regions (in some cases towns or noodle shops!) across Asia are proudly represented by their particular style of noodle and sauce, broth or toppings.

About Smith Family Retail

Smith Family Retail is a family business. We are committed to providing quality information and products to home cooks and home bakers.

Our products are distributed and sold under the Home Kitchen Queen (HKQ) brand.

HOME KITCHEN QUEEN

Smith Family Retail

Printed in Great Britain
by Amazon